"Chris Millin, placing immense value on the individual, has revolutionised the process of transformation that leads to a fulfilled life.

One's destiny is not mandated but discovered through life changing choices which empower and encourage. Chris has carefully peeled back the layers that hinder the progress of the human heart in reaching its highest goals.

This is more than just a manual or a course, or a book, or a set of excellent videos. This is an impartation from one soul to another. It is a reservoir of truth, practical and stimulating to all who participate. I highly recommend Chris Millin's work."

Dr Royree Jensen
Senior Leader, Rivers Apostolic Centre, Australia
Leader of Women on the Frontlines, Oceania

"River Flow is a fresh take on an essential subject. The course is vibrant, relevant and contemporary and is wonderfully encouraging.

River Flow presents how life has impacted us, and how we are in need of life-giving transformational change through the Holy Spirit. The presentation of practical, vitally important gospel essentials within the course certainly appeals to me.

I have no hesitation in endorsing and recommending River Flow for use in contemporary church life. Enjoy!"

David Crabtree
Founding Pastor of DaySpring Church, Castle Hill, NSW, Australia
Executive Director of UnfailingGrace Ministries, Colorado, USA

"Chris Millin is an outstanding Christian leader. His credentials flow from his determination to hear and heed what God has said.

That simple principle has led him to see signs and wonders happen in the name of Jesus in some difficult and dangerous places over many years.

His willingness to share openly and lovingly what God has shown him has gathered groups of people around the world to tune in to his weekly online teaching as well as in households and meeting places across Australia (and before that, South Africa). His relevant and accessible wisdom from God is testified to by everyone who has known him.

I commend this course to anyone who is willing to receive the impartation that will accompany these teaching sessions."

Brian Medway
National Chairman, Crosslink Christian Network, Australia

RIVER FLOW

STEP OUT IN FAITH AND FLOW LIKE A RIVER

FACILITATOR MANUAL

Created by
CHRIS MILLIN

RIVER FLOW ™
Copyright © Christopher Millin, 2021

First Edition, published 2021

Email: riverflow@jirehseed.org
URL: https://www.chrismillin.com.au

All rights reserved.
This book is protected under the copyright laws of Australia.
Without limiting the rights under copyright reserved above, no part of this publication may be reproduced, stored in or introduced into a database and retrieval system or transmitted in any form or any means (electronic, mechanical, photocopying, recording or otherwise) without the prior written permission of both the owner of copyright and the above publishers. Unless otherwise identified, Scripture references and quotations are from the New King James Version (NKJV) of the Bible.

ISBN: 978-0-6453172-3-7

Ephesians 3:4-9 NKJV

By which, when you read, you may understand my knowledge in the mystery of Christ, which in other ages was not made known to the sons of men, as it has now been revealed by the Spirit to His holy apostles and prophets: that the Gentiles should be fellow heirs, of the same body, and partakers of His promise in Christ through the gospel, of which I became a minister according to the gift of the grace of God given to me by the effective working of His power.

To me, who am less than the least of all the saints, this grace was given, that I should preach among the Gentiles the unsearchable riches of Christ, and to make all see what is the fellowship of the mystery, which from the beginning of the ages has been hidden in God who created all things through Jesus Christ;

Please scan the following QR-CODES:

RIVER FLOW VIDEO TEACHINGS
https://www.riverflowinternational.com.au/

DONATE HERE
https://donorbox.org/river-flow-support

CONTENTS

INTRODUCTION	1
IS THIS FOR YOU?	2
GROUP CONFIDENTIALITY	4
PROPOSED MEETING FORMAT	6
SESSION 1: YOUR VALUE	8
SESSION 2: TWO VOICES	14
SESSION 3: CHANGING YOUR MINDSET	22
SESSION 4: FROM HERE TO THERE	30
SESSION 5: KEEP PRESSING FORWARD	38
SESSION 6: REAL COMMUNICATION	44
SESSION 7: SETTING BOUNDARIES	52
SESSION 8: RESOLVING CONFLICT	60
SESSION 9: FLOW LIKE A RIVER	68
SESSION 10: STEPPING OUT IN FAITH	76
THANK YOU AND ADDITIONAL RESOURCES	85

INTRODUCTION

RIVER FLOW™ has been designed to lead you on a journey of self-discovery and situational awareness to a deeper freedom by unpacking a series of powerful, effective and life-changing steps. It's a springboard for change, presented in 10 transformational sessions.

RIVER FLOW™ is designed for all people, young and old, who have a desire to move from HERE to THERE.

We desire that you walk away with practical answers and a clear plan for your future. Each person is of immense value, created in the image and likeness of our Heavenly Father. If you desire to step out in faith and flow like a river, then RIVER FLOW™ is for you.

THERE IS ALWAYS HOPE
THERE IS MORE TO LIFE
YOU HAVE A CHANCE TO TRY AGAIN

This course facilitates transformation through participation, revealing key decisions to be made where individuals need encouragement by highlighting personal development areas, as well as revealing the steps of change required to transform each individual's path to their Heavenly Destiny.

Next Step: Register online for access to the RIVER FLOW™ Course Video Teachings at no extra cost www.riverflowinternational.com

IS THIS FOR YOU?

Many of us want to change our lives for the better, but we need help to highlight the things that are holding us back, and the guidance to move forward into a new and brighter destiny.

Making changes to our behaviour and lives can be very difficult.
RIVER FLOW™, will help you highlight areas in your life that are impacting you negatively and how to set a path to make changes in a way that is achievable and measurable.

RIVER FLOW™ will move you towards your intended purpose in life by unwrapping how we are shaped by circumstances around us and how certain influences potentially disable our ability to live the fruitful lives we desire to live and that our Heavenly Father has planned for us.

Each progressive session will lead you on a journey of inspirational self-discovery.

Each of us needs goals and a plan to move from where we currently are (HERE) to where we want to be (THERE).

The concept of a RIVER is used throughout as a metaphor to describe the difference between a dry, struggling, hurt and depressed land, and a land that is flourishing with life, joy, hope and opportunity. The land is our heart, and you have every right to live a life of freedom and purpose.

If you desire to move from HERE to THERE, then RIVER FLOW™ is for you.

Step out in faith and flow like a river.

GROUP CONFIDENTIALITY

For those who are doing RIVER FLOW™ course in a group setting:

As we embark on the RIVER FLOW™ journey together, we desire that the group discussions and personal thoughts shared with each other in the group sessions are respected and honoured to the highest degree.

RIVER FLOW™ is about unlocking the flow of Living Water from within. We have each been through situations that have impacted us differently and this agreement represents your desire to create a safe group environment for sharing and respect for privacy.

Please read the following statements and sign your name in agreement below:

- I understand that I may become aware of other course participant's personal and sensitive information during the RIVER FLOW™ course
- I agree to keep all personal and sensitive information shared on this course completely confidential
- I will not discuss, share or disclose any information I am privileged to, during or on completion of the course
- I agree to respect the rights of others and participate in a respectful manner
- I acknowledge that I understand my commitment to the confidentiality of personal and sensitive information and agree to the principles of this agreement

_____

(Name)

_____

(Signature)

_____

(Date)

PROPOSED MEETING FORMAT

As discussed in the Group Leadership Video, this is the proposed meeting format table.

Please also refer to the 'Three key principles for Participants to interact with each other in our meetings' … below the table.

No.	PROPOSED TIME	DESCRIPTION
0	30-minutes	Tea / Coffee / Refreshments (Suggested but Optional)
1	05-minutes	Welcome and Worship Song
2	20-minutes	Play Session Video Teaching
3	15-minutes	Group Discussion. All together. Question : "What jumped out at you during todays Session video teaching and why ?" REMEMBER … " Share from your heart in this moment " REMEMBER … Stir up discussion with your Facilitator Discussion Points
4	15-minutes	Participation Worksheet in Manual. This is a private moment to fill out the answers to the questions for each Session. Please consider playing soft worship music in the background
5	15-minutes	Break-out Groups. Try for 3-people per small group Question : " What has touched your heart during todays Session ?" REMEMBER … Share from your heart in this moment …
6	15-minutes	Group Discussion. All together. Question : "I would love to hear from you … who would like to share some highlights from your Break-out Group discussion ? " REMEMBER … Share from your heart in this moment " REMEMBER … Stir up discussion with your Facilitator Discussion Points
7	05-minutes	Play Session Video Prayer
	90-minutes	Excluding Tea / Coffee / Refreshments
	120-minutes	Including Tea / Coffee / Refreshments

Three key principles for participants to interact with each other in our meetings.

- Firstly, 'To share and not to tell',

- Secondly, we ask Group Participants 'to keep focussed on the Session at hand', and

- Last but not least, to give everyone in the group a voice in the discussions'

SESSION 1: YOUR VALUE

"YOU ARE WONDERFULLY MADE"

They tried to bury us,
They didn't know we were seeds ...

For I can do everything through Christ, who gives me strength.

Philippians 4:13

SESSION 1: YOUR VALUE

OBJECTIVES

- ❖ To see yourself with a fresh perspective
- ❖ You are uniquely and wonderfully made
- ❖ You are important and you are of great value

KEY CONCEPTS

- ❖ You can't change your past, but you can shape your future
- ❖ If you continue to do what you've always done, you will continue to get the same results
- ❖ You must <u>choose</u> to start today
- ❖ Each seed has a place and a purpose
- ❖ Each of us is a unique seed ready to take part in life

From the time we are born until now, we are influenced (shaped) by:

- ❖ People
- ❖ Places
- ❖ Circumstances
- ❖ Things

These influences are like SOIL and NUTRIENTS that surrounds a seed.

These different influences come into our lives in different ways:

- ❖ Willingly (by choice, even if by poor choices)
- ❖ Unwillingly (forced on us)
- ❖ Knowingly (we are aware of them)
- ❖ Unknowingly (we are unaware of them)

SESSION 1: YOUR VALUE

 PARTICIPATION

Which one of the following indicates where you are at with your past:

- ☐ I can't face my past yet
- ☐ I'm starting to face my past but it's hard to understand
- ☐ I understand my past, and I'm beginning to deal with things
- ☐ I am ready to move on

Write 3 GOOD things that you like about yourself and are positive (be kind to yourself...)

1. _____
2. _____
3. _____

Write 3 things about your PAST that you are still dealing with today

1. _____
2. _____
3. _____

Write 3 things about you that you believe must change in order to move forward

1. _____
2. _____
3. _____

SESSION 1: YOUR VALUE

 SCRIPTURES

Genesis 1:26
Then God said, "Let Us make man in Our image, according to Our likeness ...

Jeremiah 29:11
For I know the thoughts that I think toward you, says the LORD, thoughts of peace and not of evil, to give you a future and a hope.

John 3:30
He must increase, but I must decrease.

1 Peter 1:15-16
but as He who called you is holy, you also be holy in all your conduct, because it is written, "Be holy, for I am holy."

 FACILITATOR DISCUSSION POINTS

- Each of us are influenced by circumstances around us
- These things have tried to bury you, but they didn't know you were a SEED
- Shake off the past and look up
- You must accept that things have happened in your past that you cannot change but you can change your future
- There is a force within you that contains all you need to flourish
- A seed is packed with everything it needs to reach its full potential
- A seed grows from the inside out
- We cannot grow from the outside in
- A seed needs the right soil in which to flourish
- A seed needs water to grow
- A seed needs light to grow
- A seed may be planted in the wrong place
- It may need different nutrients
- It may need new life

SESSION 1: YOUR VALUE

 **PRAYER**

HEAVENLY FATHER,

Inside me You have placed something unique and wonderful.

Help me to be free from the things inside me that hold me back.

I have been created in Your image and likeness.

I actually look like You,

I am wonderfully made,

Inside me You have planted a Heavenly Destiny.

I so desire to understand my true value,

to see the seed of Hope You have placed within me,

to grow and be fruitful in all things.

I can do this, with Your help …

Help me Lord with the strength to become who You made me to be

My life has had so many ups and downs.

Help the soil of my heart to strengthen and be healthy and be

ready to receive what You have for me.

Water and nourish the seed of who You made me to be.

Help me to see the value You have placed inside me.

I step forward today, embarking on a magnificent journey with You.

I give You my heart.

Let my River Flow.

In Jesus Name

AMEN

SESSION 1: YOUR VALUE

 NOTES

Please use the space below to write down comments, thoughts, ideas, pictures etc …as our Heavenly Father shows you important things for your life…

SESSION 2: TWO VOICES

"CHOOSE THE VOICE OF THE LORD"

Jesus said, "I am the light of the world. If you follow me, you won't have to walk in darkness, because you will have the light that leads to life."

John 8:12

SESSION 2: TWO VOICES

OBJECTIVES

- To recognise that there are 'two voices' that try to speak to us
- One wants to break you down, the other wants to see you lifted up
- It's important to listen to the voice that leads you to Joy

KEY CONCEPTS

- LIGHT is greater than darkness
- Darkness may surround us but Light is stronger
- Darkness brings hopelessness
- Light brings Hope
- We need Light in order to grow
- There are two voices fighting for your attention: good/light and evil/darkness

Examples of the influences that SPEAK into our lives (good and bad influences)

- People (family, friends, strangers, teachers, colleagues, bosses …)
- TV
- Social media
- Magazines, books
- Past experiences

Examples of the negative voices that bring darkness into your life:

- You are just like your father / mother / brother / sister
- You are worthless
- What is the point in trying?
- You can never change your life
- It's too late
- You cannot change
- You are not strong/smart enough
- I hate you

Examples of positive voices that bring LIGHT into your life:

- You are uniquely made and carry greatness inside you
- You are truly amazing
- You are a Champion
- It's never too late
- I believe in you
- You can do this
- You can change your life
- You are stronger than you think
- I love you

SESSION 2: TWO VOICES

 PARTICIPATION

Tick below where people have spoken negatively into your life:

- ☐ Someone in my family (write their names below)
  _____

- ☐ Friends I used to hang out with or grew up with (write their names below)
  _____

- ☐ A past relationship (write their name/s below)
  _____

- ☐ A current relationship (write their name/s below)
  _____

- ☐ Someone from a job I used to work at (write their name/s below)
  _____

- ☐ A teacher or educator (write their name/s below)
  _____

KEY: Understanding their perspective, understanding your value and limiting their influence on you

Tick the following areas that are influencing you negatively

- ☐ TV
- ☐ Games (online, X-box, iPad, etc …)
- ☐ Mobile phone
- ☐ Social media
- ☐ Books, magazines, movies
- ☐ Other (list) _____

KEY: It's important to know what is real and what is fake, understanding your value, limiting their influence on you

Write 3 POSITIVE things that you have heard others say about you

_____

_____

_____

SESSION 2: TWO VOICES

 SCRIPTURES:

John 1:1-5
In the beginning was the Word, and the Word was with God, and the Word was God. He was in the beginning with God. All things were made through Him, and without Him nothing was made that was made. In Him was life, and the life was the light of men. And the light shines in the darkness, and the darkness did not comprehend it.

Proverbs 23:7
For as he (a person) thinks in his heart, so is he (are they) ...

John 10:10
The thief (satan/enemy of God) does not come except to steal, and to kill, and to destroy. I (JESUS) have come that they (YOU /ME) may have life, and that they may have it more abundantly.

Psalms 23:1-3
The LORD is my shepherd;
I shall not want.
He makes me to lie down in green pastures;
He leads me beside the still waters.
He restores my soul;
He leads me in the paths of righteousness
For His name's sake.

 FACILITATOR DISCUSSION POINTS

- When Light shines, darkness runs away
- We must consciously decide to cut off the negative voices that are influencing us
- We must choose to be a positive voice to those around us, to bring life and light to them
- When someone lies about you or says things about you that are not true, does it really matter?
- It's important to know the truth about ourselves and ignore the lies
- Actions speak louder than words (show them who you are by your actions)
- Some people don't like it when you decide to make more out of your life
- They may try to pull you back to who you used to be, hold tight to your future and choose to believe in the Lord and in yourself
- Joy and happiness are different, Joy is a spiritual fruit, and always accompanied by supernatural peace

SESSION 2: TWO VOICES

 PRAYER

HEAVENLY FATHER,

For too long I have allowed negative words to hurt me.

I realise now that darkness and light are calling me at the same time.

The enemy of God is trying to deceive me,

and lead me astray so I will struggle and fail.

But the LORD's voice is a shining light to guide me to Truth.

I have at times listened to the wrong voice and allowed it to control my thoughts and actions.

Lord you are the Good Shepherd and You promise to lead me to good places.

Your sheep know Your Voice,

and You know Your sheep by name.

Shine Your brilliant light on my path ahead.

Your Light drives out darkness.

Forgive me for listening to and believing the wrong influences.

Forgive me for participating in things I know are wrong.

I no longer want to be led astray.

I desire to be on track, with You.

Help me to tune into Your Voice.

I surrender to You Lord and I take my stand against all darkness and deception.

You have come to bring Life in abundance.

I am who You say I am,

help me to be FREE.

Help me to tune into Your heart.

In Jesus Name

AMEN

SESSION 2: TWO VOICES

 NOTES

Please use the space below to write down comments, thoughts, ideas, pictures etc …as our Heavenly Father shows you important things for your life…

SESSION 3: CHANGING YOUR MINDSET

"YOU CAN BE RENEWED"

Don't copy the behaviour and customs of this world, but let God transform you into a new person by changing the way you think.

Romans 12:2

SESSION 3: CHANGING YOUR MINDSET

OBJECTIVES

- Defining a Glass Wall (mindset limitation / blind spot)
- Recognising that our wrong mindsets can hold us hostage
- Your current mindset can be changed / renewed

KEY CONCEPTS

- We each have different ways we have developed
- Different life experiences can shape our minds
- The way we think and process information is not the same as each other
- How we grow up and develop can bring freedom or constraints to our thinking
- We are not always aware of how our mindsets are limiting our choices
- Blind spots are things we don't know are there
- These blind spots are like Glass Walls inside our mind that structure how we think
- We call them Glass Walls because often we don't know that they are there, until we bump into them
- When we press the paradigm of our thinking, we often bump into internal resistance we never knew was there
- It's hard to put into words the resistance to certain things we know are needed (good for us) and yet we can't seem to break through / overcome

Here are some things that can create Glass Walls in our thinking, and hold us hostage, if we let them:

- How we grew up with our families (structure, influence, hurts, finances)
- Our unique traditions (different cultures)
- Education
- Opportunities
- Fears / threats (loneliness, violence, attacks, abuse, bullying, sickness, addictions, mental-health …)
- Past mistakes
- Circumstances out of your control
- Tragedy (past devastation that has hurt you and/or your loved ones)

Keys to how you can create a new mind within you:

- Be prepared to do things differently
- Challenge the ways things 'were always done'
- Be secure in who you are and be open to change
- Be disciplined in the changes you know you must make to achieve to your dream
- It's never too late
- The LORD is able to help you to change your thinking and heal your mind
- Trust your Heavenly Father to transform your blind spots, break down Glass Walls and renew your mind

SESSION 3: CHANGING YOUR MINDSET

 PARTICIPATION

Which statements below best describe your current Glass Walls situation

- ☐ I recognise that my mindset needs the Glass Walls to come down
- ☐ I want to be free from limitations
- ☐ I want to change, but I don't know how
- ☐ I can and will change, I'm ready to do this

For you personally, list what you think needs to change in your thinking

- Write down repeat situations that end up causing you pain and/or loss
- Consider your dream and the Glass Walls that are in your way
- Perhaps it's something you wish you did not do
- Remember that the first step in smashing the Glass Walls is shining light on it, by writing it down

_____
_____
_____
_____
_____
_____
_____
_____
_____
_____
_____
_____

SESSION 3: CHANGING YOUR MINDSET

 SCRIPTURES:

Romans 12:2 (NASB)
And do not be conformed to this world, but be transformed by the renewing of your mind, that you may prove what is that good and acceptable and perfect will of God.

Romans 12:2 (NLT)
Don't copy the behaviour and customs of this world, but let God transform you into a new person by changing the way you think.

Isaiah 54:17
No weapon formed against you shall prosper,
And every tongue which rises against you in judgment; You shall condemn...

2 Timothy 1:7
For God has not given us a spirit of fear, but of power and of love and of a sound mind.

Titus 3:5
not by works of righteousness which we have done, but according to His mercy He saved us, through the washing of regeneration and renewing of the Holy Spirit,

1 Corinthians 2:16
For "who has known the mind of the LORD that he may instruct Him?" But we have the mind of Christ.

 FACILITATOR DISCUSSION POINTS:

Briefly discuss the power of the mind in relation to:

- Having a Positive Mental Attitude (taking MYSELF forward)
- Having a Negative Mental Attitude (holding MYSELF back)
- Having the mind of Christ (being transformed by the renewing of your mind)
- Blind spots need to be highlighted in order to overcome them
- Glass Walls come down when we are prepared to put pressure on blind spots
- Your desire to change must be great, fuelled by the vision you have to be stronger, better and more in alignment with the dream of your heart
- Wrong mindsets can hold us back, hold us hostage and limit our future
- Your current mindset can be changed / renewed
- The <u>desire to change</u> is the catalyst for transformation
- The mere act of shining light (Light of Jesus) on the problem, becomes a hammer to the Glass Walls

SESSION 3: CHANGING YOUR MINDSET

 PRAYER

HEAVENLY FATHER,

There are things that I know need to change in my thinking.

I have further to go in my understanding.

Glass walls are in my way and are holding me back.

Areas of my thinking that have become blind spots,

and need to be renewed by your Truth.

I ask you for help Lord,

to highlight and shine your Light, into my mind, my thoughts,

my understanding, my behaviours, and attitudes.

Things have happened to me that have caused me to be shaped this way.

I learned today that You can help my mind to be transformed.

Heavenly Father, Heal my mind …

Jesus You are the Way, the Truth and the Life.

My mind can be renewed by You,

washed by Your Truth.

Renew my mind in Jesus Name.

I lay down all fear at your feet.

Help me establish a new and disciplined mind.

As Glass Walls come down and blind spots are removed,

help me to have a mind like Yours.

In Jesus Name

AMEN

SESSION 3: CHANGING YOUR MINDSET

 NOTES

Please use the space below to write down comments, thoughts, ideas, pictures etc …as our Heavenly Father shows you important things for your life…

SESSION 4: FROM HERE TO THERE

"SEE A NEW FUTURE THROUGH JESUS"

looking unto Jesus, the author and finisher of our faith…
Hebrews 12:2

SESSION 4: FROM HERE TO THERE

OBJECTIVES

- How to change your reality into your Destiny
- Recognising your current position in contrast to your desired (future) destination
- Practical way to taking your first Step to Freedom

KEY CONCEPTS

- HERE is where you are right now
- THERE is where you desire to be
- Your Heavenly Destiny is the destiny that the Lord has planned for you
- To desire your Heavenly Destiny, to come into agreement with His path for you
- Oftentimes, the path between HERE and THERE seems massive and almost impossible to traverse
- We see a vision of where we want to be, but we can't find the strength to fulfil our dreams
- We see the tree that needs to be climbed and often we are stretching for a branch that is too high, when there is a branch lower down that we can grab and use it to take a step closer to our dream

KEYS to releasing your Destiny:

- Every journey starts with a single step
- Set goals and take small steps in the direction of your dream
- Discipline and focus are needed to remain on track
- Faith in yourself and the dream given to you will drive you forward
- Pride keeps us back
- Humility takes us forward
- Humbling ourselves in order to be lifted up by Him
- Small achievable steps (Here to There) is progress
- Many small steps make up the journey
- Small steps allow you to accomplish objectives and builds self-worth
- Once momentum builds you will be unstoppable

Voices to consider when you step out from HERE to THERE:

- **Fear** says "I can't do it"
- **Pride** says "I won't do it, it's beneath me"
- **Arrogance** says "Whatever"
- **Jealousy** says "Do you think you are better than us"
- **Love** says "You can do it"
- **Focus**, urgency and necessity says "I must do what it takes"
- **Humility** says "I will do what it takes"
- **Faith** says "Don't give up"
- **Discipline** says "One step at a time"
- **Grace** says "You are worthy to do this"
- **Healing** says "I am no longer who I used to be, I am a new creation"

SESSION 4: FROM HERE TO THERE

 PARTICIPATION

Tick which of the following reflects what you are FEELING when it comes to your desired destiny. It's important to acknowledge your feelings, to reflect on your current position (your HERE):

- ☐ Nervous / Scared / Fearful
- ☐ Intimidated
- ☐ Depressed
- ☐ Excited / Joyful
- ☐ I can do this
- ☐ Freedom is on its way
- ☐ It is time to do this
- ☐ Other _____ (write)

Expanding on the question above, describe your current situation and where you are at right now:

- _____
- _____
- _____

Describe your desired future situation and where you DESIRE TO BE:

- _____
- _____
- _____

What can you commit to doing in order to move towards your HEAVENLY DESTINY

- _____
- _____
- _____

SESSION 4: FROM HERE TO THERE

 SCRIPTURES

Proverbs 3:5-6
Trust in the LORD with all your heart, And lean not on your own understanding;
In all your ways acknowledge Him, And He shall direct your paths.

Jeremiah 17:7
Blessed is the man (person) who trusts in the LORD, And whose hope is the LORD.

Philippians 1:6
being confident of this very thing, that He who has begun a good work in you will complete it until the day of Jesus Christ;

Romans 8:28
And we know that all things work together for good to those who love God, to those who are the called according to His purpose.

Philippians 3:14
I press toward the goal for the prize of the upward call of God in Christ Jesus.

Hebrews 12:2
looking unto Jesus, the author and finisher of our faith...

 FACILITATOR DISCUSSION POINTS:

These are practical examples to unpack the importance of being honest about where you are at right now (HERE) as well as where you desire to be (THERE)

- Discuss using GOOGLE MAPS or any other GPS, map or navigation apps
- In order to get directions, there are **two key pieces of information needed**, firstly, your current position (HERE) and secondly, your desired destination (THERE)
- Many of us know where we want to be … the problem is that we are not being honest about our current position
- The navigation app will not give directions until your current position is clear
- It's critical to establish what your reality is right now, so you don't keep hiding but face up to the RIGHT NOW VIEW of your life
- Knowing where you are now (HERE) is critical, but also need to know where it is that you want to go (THERE)
- The closer you get to your destination, the more accurate your directions need to be, or else you will keep circling, and never get THERE

SESSION 4: FROM HERE TO THERE

 PRAYER

HEAVENLY FATHER,

You know the way forward for me.

You made me and You can guide me,

at times I have gone off track,

causing me to lose my direction and lose sight of You Lord.

As I step forward bravely and take hold of my very own Heavenly Destiny

Thank you that You receive me just as I am.

Thank you for not giving up on me,

and keeping the door open for me.

Thank you that You are the One who authors and perfects my faith

You multiply my faith capacity.

Even though I am taking new steps forward,

I realise that I am not alone.

With You I can do incredible things.

I can achieve things beyond my imagination.

As I take Your hand today,

Shift my destiny LORD …

Forgive me for trying to do this without You.

Lead me …

Guide me …

Establish me …

I am ready to take this next step with You.

In Jesus Name

AMEN

SESSION 4: FROM HERE TO THERE

 NOTES

Please use the space below to write down comments, thoughts, ideas, pictures etc …as our Heavenly Father shows you important things for your life…

SESSION 5: KEEP PRESSING FORWARD

"THROUGH FAITH YOU CAN DO THE IMPOSSIBLE"

… rivers of living water will flow from your heart.

John 7:38

SESSION 5: KEEP PRESSING FORWARD

OBJECTIVES

- Feedback session
- Give everyone a chance to speak
- Share highlights so far

KEY CONCEPTS

- Each session is another step towards your goals
- You have each challenged yourselves to change
- It's been emotional and difficult at times
- Old patterns, mindsets and behaviours have been highlighted
- Lasting change is possible
- You can change your future
- Changing how you think about yourself
- Interacting differently with others
- Choosing who you interact with
- Believe in yourself
- Increase in Faith
- Re-alignment to the Lord Jesus Christ and His plan for you
- Clean hands and a pure heart
- He makes us into a new creation

Closing for the day:

- Thank you for being so brave to set a new path for your life
- You have taken important steps towards your freedom
- Congratulations we are halfway there, see you next session

SESSION 5: KEEP PRESSING FORWARD

 PARTICIPATION

Please answer the following questions briefly:

Q1 – What have you noticed today about yourself that you didn't know before?

_____
_____
_____
_____
_____

Q2 – What encouragement have you received today?

_____
_____
_____
_____
_____

Q3 – What changes will you be making going forward?

_____
_____
_____
_____
_____

SESSION 5: KEEP PRESSING FORWARD

 SCRIPTURES

Ephesians 4:23
and be renewed in the spirit of your mind,

Ephesians 4:24
and that you put on the new man which was created according to God, in true righteousness and holiness.

Proverbs 27:19
As in water face reflects face,
So a man's heart reveals the man.
(So a person's heart reveals the person, man = mankind)

Psalms 24:3-4
Who may ascend into the hill of the LORD?
Or who may stand in His holy place?
He who has clean hands and a pure heart,
Who has not lifted up his soul to an idol,
Nor sworn deceitfully.

1 Peter 5:7
casting all your care (burdens) upon Him, for He cares for you.

John 7:38
He who believes in Me, as the Scripture has said, out of his heart will flow rivers of living water.

 FACILITATOR DISCUSSION POINTS

This is an opportunity to talk about making a fresh commitment to the Lord Jesus

- ❖ Some will be feeling burdened by the weight of needing to change their ways
- ❖ Talk them through the following 2 x scriptures
    - ▸ Romans 10:13 : For "<u>whoever</u> calls on the name of the LORD shall be saved."
    - ▸ 1 John 3:3 : And <u>everyone</u> who has this hope in Him purifies himself, just as He is pure.
- ❖ Emphasise: no sin is greater than the Blood of Jesus and His Sacrifice for each of us
- ❖ Emphasise: <u>whoever</u> and <u>everyone</u> includes us ALL

SESSION 5: KEEP PRESSING FORWARD

 PRAYER

Note: During this prayer, there will be a time of silent reflection and handing over.

Name each burden and sin, handing them over to our Loving Father

Picture yourself giving them to Him; do this silently in your heart.

HEAVENLY FATHER,

There are things that I know need to change in my thinking.

You are the One, leading me to change my ways.

To be transformed by the renewing of my mind.

Thank you that You gave Your life for me,

that You died on the Cross,

so that I can live a new life through You.

I ask forgiveness for the resistance in my heart.

I ask forgiveness for my sins.

(TIME OF SILENT REFLECTION AND HANDING OVER)

I hand You my past,

the things I cannot change, are Yours now Lord …

I lay the burdens of my heart before You.

Thank you for making a way through all this … for me, personally.

Thank you for Your forgiveness,

for washing my hands and giving me a new heart,

for giving me a fresh start.

May clear and crystal rivers of Living Water,

flow from You to me … fill me Lord.

Let Living Waters flow out of me to those around me.

In Jesus Name

AMEN

SESSION 5: KEEP PRESSING FORWARD

 NOTES

Please use the space below to write down comments, thoughts, ideas, pictures etc …as our Heavenly Father shows you important things for your life…

SESSION 6: REAL COMMUNICATION

"PRESENT YOURSELF WELL"

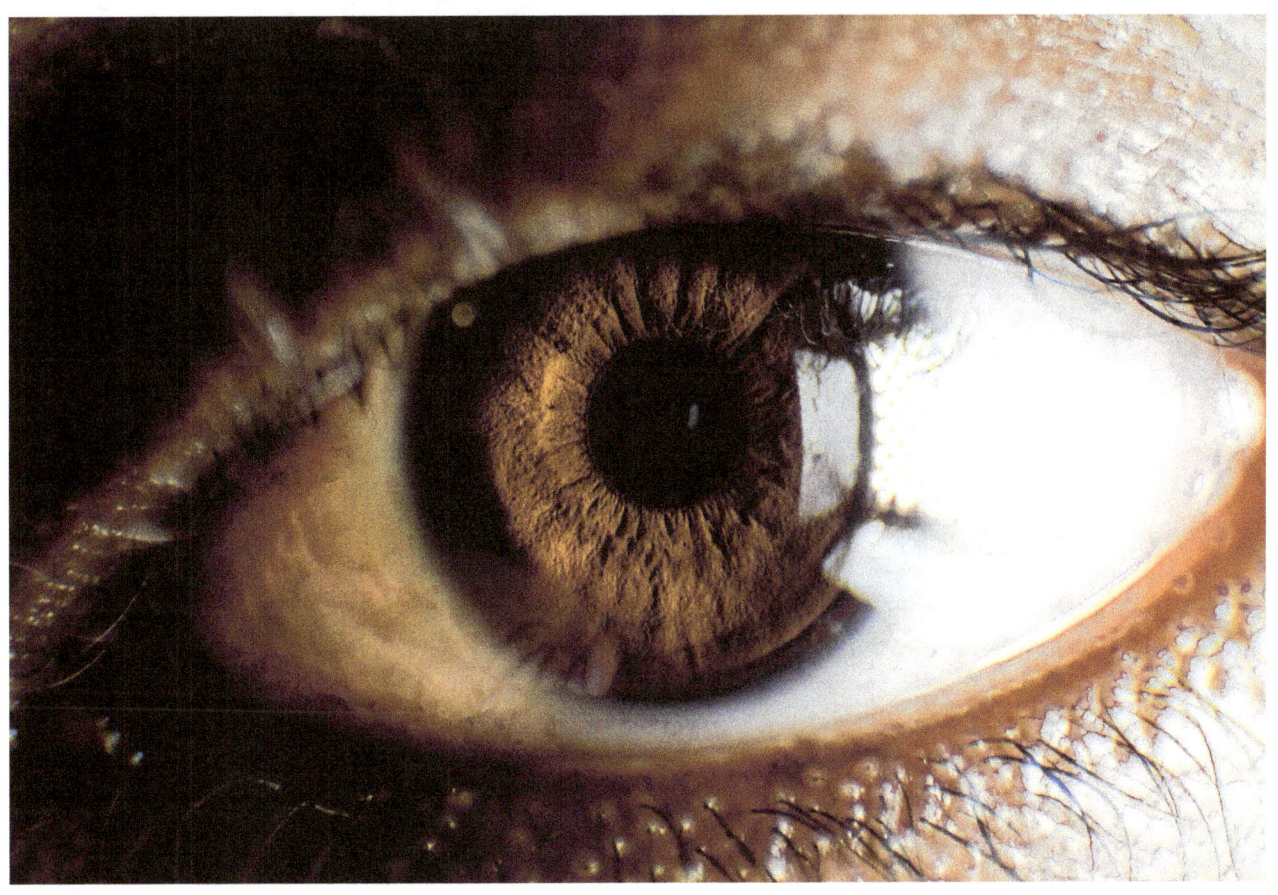

Your eye is like a lamp that provides light for your body. When your eye is healthy, your whole body is filled with light.

Matthew 6:22

SESSION 6: REAL COMMUNICATION

OBJECTIVES

- ❖ The importance of communicating effectively to represent yourself well
- ❖ Speech, attitude and body language
- ❖ Personal appearance and hygiene

KEY CONCEPTS

- ❖ People communicate in many ways
- ❖ Speech is how we use language and is a main form of communication, but it's not our only means of communication
- ❖ It's important to understand that how we look, speak and act leave an impression on others
- ❖ Future opportunities can be unlocked as we project the right self-image
- ❖ Poor personal hygiene can negatively impact your relationships and opportunities
- ❖ Verbal and non-verbal communication is important
- ❖ Enabling others to have confidence in you by doing what you say
- ❖ Let your yes be yes and your no be no
- ❖ It's important to acknowledge and honour cultural differences to communication
- ❖ Being careful to speak about others in a way you would want them to talk about you (guard against gossiping)
- ❖ The eyes (and ears) are the 'window of the soul'
- ❖ What you put in your mind, your brain will process, and ultimately influences your thoughts and words
- ❖ Your tone-of-voice influences how you say what you want to say (speaking softly vs. loudly)
- ❖ Your choice of words are important (e.g. saying … whatever… vs. yes please…)

The following are examples of things that can influence the way you communicate (good and bad influences)

- ❖ People we interact with / Social gatherings
- ❖ TV / Movies
- ❖ Magazines / Social media
- ❖ Substances we consume: Alcohol / Drugs
- ❖ Sport
- ❖ Online gaming
- ❖ News
- ❖ Other _____

You can change the way you communicate (behaviour) by doing these TWO things:

- ❖ <u>Choosing to do things differently</u>: making a firm choice that you want to change, for you and those around you
- ❖ <u>Changing your inputs</u> and the negative influences in your life

SESSION 6: REAL COMMUNICATION

 PARTICIPATION

Tick the following that are NEGATIVE INPUTS in your life, that need to change:

- ☐ TV / Movies
- ☐ Social gatherings
- ☐ Alcohol / Drugs
- ☐ Gaming
- ☐ Magazines / Social media
- ☐ People
- ☐ News
- ☐ Other _____ (write other things here)

Select either YES or NO for each statement below:

YES	NO	
___	___	I speak clearly and confidently
___	___	I choose my words carefully
___	___	I am well-mannered and polite
___	___	I take care to present myself well
___	___	I believe how I dress represents my desired future (dressed for success)
___	___	My personal hygiene is great
___	___	I am careful not to talk about others negatively behind their back (gossip)
___	___	I can see that how I communicate affects how others see me
___	___	I understand that how others see me, can impact my opportunities in life
___	___	I can see that my behaviour can influence others negatively or positively
___	___	I can change the way I communicate to others more positively

SESSION 6: REAL COMMUNICATION

 SCRIPTURES

James 1:19
My dear brothers and sisters, take note of this: Everyone should be quick to listen, slow to speak and slow to become angry

Proverbs 15:1
A gentle answer turns away wrath, but a harsh word stirs up anger.

Psalms 141:3
Set a guard over my mouth, LORD; keep watch over the door of my lips.

Matthew 6:22
"The lamp of the body is the eye. If therefore your eye is good, your whole body will be full of light.

1 Thessalonians 5:11
Therefore encourage one another and build each other up, just as in fact you are doing.

Proverbs 18:21
Death and life are in the power of the tongue, And those who love it will eat its fruit.

Psalms 19:14
Let the words of my mouth and the meditation of my heart
Be acceptable in Your sight, O LORD, my strength and my Redeemer.

Luke 6:45
A good man brings good things out of the good stored up in his heart, and an evil man brings evil things out of the evil stored up in his heart. For the mouth speaks what the heart is full of.

SESSION 6: REAL COMMUNICATION

 FACILITATOR DISCUSSION POINTS

Briefly discuss the power of the mind in relation to:

- ❖ In order to change your pattern of communication you must discuss the link between INPUTS and OUTPUT
- ❖ INPUTS are what goes into your mind, through your interactions (eyes, ears, mind, thoughts, memories, etc.)
- ❖ OUTPUTS are what comes out of your mind, as you interact with others (words, actions, behaviours, attitudes, etc.)
- ❖ Negative inputs = negative outputs
- ❖ Positive inputs = positive outputs
- ❖ PEOPLE can be positive inputs and/or negative inputs

Question:

Have you even noticed that we often change depending on who we hang around with?

- ❖ Discuss real examples of positive and negative INPUTS
- ❖ Discuss real examples of positive and negative OUTPUTS
- ❖ Setting rules and boundaries for the inputs in your life is important, you must be in charge of yourself
- ❖ You must change your way of responding to things (INPUTS)
- ❖ You must renew your mind to respond differently (Romans 12:2)
- ❖ You must learn new patterns to communicate and represent yourself differently (OUTPUTS)

SESSION 6: REAL COMMUNICATION

 PRAYER

HEAVENLY FATHER,

    I lift up my life to You, Lord,

    how I communicate and interact with others,

    how I represent myself to others,

    And how I represent You…

    I ask You to help me, Lord

    with my thoughts, my words and my actions.

    Help me with my interactions with others and my input into their lives.

    I ask LORD that You forgive me,

    for resisting what is good and right in Your eyes.

    Lead me forward as I take Your hand,

    to change my ways from the inside out and the outside in.

    Help me to be conscious of what I allow into my life

    Help me to be conscious of how things affect my heart

    and how I represent myself … and impact those around me.

    Help me to be conscious of what comes out of my heart,

    and out of my mouth

    I acknowledge today that I must be careful

    and guard what I allow into my heart.

    Cleanse me and refresh me by Your Spirit.

    Give me strength to change my ways, for good.

    Thank you for leading me to the best outcome for me.

    Let me be clothed in Your Light.

    Let me shine from the inside out.

    In Jesus Name

AMEN

SESSION 6: REAL COMMUNICATION

 NOTES

Please use the space below to write down comments, thoughts, ideas, pictures etc …as our Heavenly Father shows you important things for your life…

SESSION 7: SETTING BOUNDARIES

"FIND REST AND REPLENISHMENT"

For my yoke is easy to bear, and the burden I give you is light.

Matthew 11:30

SESSION 7: SETTING BOUNDARIES

OBJECTIVES

- Acknowledging the human need for safety and replenishment
- Voicing and setting personal boundaries allow others to understand your needs
- Setting clear ground rules for your own replenishment
- Boundaries need to be established regarding your behaviour and what you allow to influence you
- Boundaries also need to be established for how you give others access to you and how they influence you

KEY CONCEPTS

- In this session, the concept of your INNER RIVER is a picture of your spiritual, physical and emotional energy
- Some of us feel like we have no energy left, our cup is empty
- Others have energy but are being pulled in many different directions but never fully replenish
- Most of us leave our own needs to last
- Or worse we just forget about our own needs, giving without getting anything back
- A river without banks is a swamp, it spreads everywhere
- Our energy can be dispersed in many directions resulting in fatigue (exhaustion), depression or anxiety
- When you give more than what is coming in, over time there will be a consequence
- The world is demanding more and more of your energy, focus and time (time is money, right?)
- Cost of living is increasing and personal space is decreasing
- You need boundaries in your life, to ensure your inner river flows strong
- Boundaries are like channels that make sure you flow strongly in the right direction
- By setting your INNER RIVERBANKS in position, you can effectively keep your Inner river energy flowing
- Riverbanks (boundaries) protect you and keep you from spreading yourself too thin
- It's easy to lose touch with yourself and your reality
- It's not selfish to need personal space
- You also need the right people in your life

Our INNER RIVER energy can be:

- Physical (Body)
- Emotional (Soul)
- Spiritual (Spirit)
- All working together, interconnected, as one
- Your source of replenishment is Living Water
- Living Water within flows from the Spirit … Spirit, Soul, Body

Many people try to escape their current reality by trying to switch off their mind:

- By engaging harmful behaviours
- Being too tired to say NO
- Separating or withdrawing from others
- Shutting down communication
- Overeating, substance abuse, gambling, other addictions…
- Having the wrong people and relationships in your life
- Escaping responsibility, hiding away, not facing your reality

SESSION 7: SETTING BOUNDARIES

 PARTICIPATION

Balance is important for your personal replenishment, tick which of the following you enjoy:
- [ ] Being alone
- [ ] Being with trusted (close) friends
- [ ] Rest
- [ ] Sunlight
- [ ] Exercise
- [ ] Being quiet
- [ ] Being in nature
- [ ] Eating well
- [ ] Having time to think
- [ ] Other _____

Do you personally STRUGGLE with the following?
Select either YES or NO for each statement below:

YES	NO	
___	___	Fatigue (exhaustion, tiredness) depression, anxiety
___	___	Alcohol, drugs, overeating, substance abuse, gambling, other addictions
___	___	Too much time gaming or on social media
___	___	Lack of focus, procrastination
___	___	Anger, control, manipulation, frustration, irritation, jealousy, disappointment
___	___	Escapism / not facing your reality: movies, books, social media etc.
___	___	Hurt, resentment, unforgiveness

List how many hours a day you spend on the following:

Q1 - Time with yourself in a quiet place recharging   _____ (hours)

Q2 - TV, movies, gaming, social media, screen time   _____ (hours)

Q3 - Studying, planning and investing time in your future   _____ (hours)

Q4 - Connecting with your Heavenly Father   _____ (hours)

Q5 - With all technology off, including your phone   _____ (hours)

Q6 - Sleep during nighttime   _____ (hours)

Q7 - Sleep during daytime   _____ (hours)

SESSION 7: SETTING BOUNDARIES

 SCRIPTURES

Psalms 23:2-3
He makes me to lie down in green pastures;
He leads me beside the still waters.
He restores my soul;
He leads me in the paths of righteousness, For His name's sake.

Psalms 23:5
You prepare a table before me in the presence of my enemies;
You anoint my head with oil; My cup runs over.

John 4:13-14
Jesus answered and said to her, "Whoever drinks of this water will thirst again, but whoever drinks of the water that I shall give him will never thirst. But the water that I shall give him will become in him a fountain of water springing up into everlasting life."

Jeremiah 31:25
For I have satiated the weary soul, and I have replenished every sorrowful soul."

1 Chronicles 16:11
Seek the LORD and His strength; Seek His face evermore!

Isaiah 40:31
But those who wait on the LORD, Shall renew their strength …

 EXERCISE

Exercise: Entering Fathers' stillness : 5-minute replenishment

Please make time to do this exercise as a group.

You are encouraged to keep doing this on your own, as often as you need to.

1. <u>Close your eyes</u> and quiet down to enable a calm spiritual state of mind
2. Still your thoughts, focus on your Heavenly Father, let Him BREATHE LIFE into you
3. Stop all thoughts that are distracting you
4. Settle and rest in Him, see yourself as He sees you, perfect Love casts out fear …
5. When you make this connection, you feel grounded
6. There may be time to review how individuals experienced divinely connecting to our Heavenly Fathers stillness … calm waters … living waters … replenishment

SESSION 7: SETTING BOUNDARIES

 FACILITATOR DISCUSSION POINTS:

Discuss the following points:

- You can't Just keep taking money from your bank account if you put nothing back, you will run out or go into debt
- We must understand that we are spiritual beings and need spiritual replenishment
- Spirit (Spiritual), Soul (Emotional), Body (Physical)
- Our 'inner river' needs to flow cleanly and freely … 'clean hands and a pure heart'
- Look to your Heavenly Father to fill you, He promises to give you Living Water
- We all need to 'reset' ourselves, to gain a fresh perspective, like a re-boot of our inner-being

Exercise: Lead the Participants in: Entering Fathers' stillness : 5-minute replenishment

- Entering Fathers' stillness : 5-minute replenishment
- Afterwards, encourage Participants to write down words, thoughts, visions, pictures … that surface during this exercise

SESSION 7: SETTING BOUNDARIES

 **PRAYER**

HEAVENLY FATHER,

Teach me to connect to Your divine flow of Living Water,

to be replenished, filled-up … restored.

Help me to have strong inner river banks.

To flow and not run out …

There are things that I know I need to change in my thinking and behaviour.

So many things try and distract me from what I know I need to do.

Your presence is beautiful and replenishing.

You are a deep fountain of life giving Living Water.

I so thirst for You, for the safety of Your protection.

You promise me a future that is bright …

I really want to believe that I can have the future You have prepared for me.

So much works against me to take me off track.

Lord, I am so worthy of the future You have for me.

You have paid a great price for me to be worthy of a brilliant future

Forgive me for losing hope and feeling unworthy of Your Love.

It's like I avoid things because I struggle to feel worthy of the good things You have for me.

Help me to establish the right boundaries, to protect myself,

so I can flourish, and be my best.

Help me to be established and be on track with what's important.

Pour out Your Living Water on me, in me and through me …

Breathe out Your Living Breath.

Fill me up again, and again.

As I rest in You my LORD …

(Encourage a still, quiet moment with eyes still closed, before closing the prayer)

AMEN

SESSION 7: SETTING BOUNDARIES

 NOTES

Please use the space below to write down comments, thoughts, ideas, pictures etc …as our Heavenly Father shows you important things for your life…

SESSION 8: RESOLVING CONFLICT

"HEAL SEPARATION THROUGH FORGIVENESS"

The Lord is gracious and compassionate; slow to anger and great in mercy.

Psalm 145:8

SESSION 8: RESOLVING CONFLICT

OBJECTIVES

- There is always more than one perspective
- Listening to hear and not react
- Taking time to think before making decisions
- Not taking offence and forgiving others is key

KEY CONCEPTS

- Conflict happens between people and can result in relationships being harmed
- There are so many differing paths and opinions to what is right and wrong, that conflict with others is almost unavoidable
- Particularly when you have chosen to follow Jesus ...
- Many will disagree with you, and you will perhaps disagree with them
- We must allow new behaviours to bring LIFE to the potential relational breakdowns caused by conflict
- Listening intentionally to hear and understand, not just to react
- Reacting is linked to defending yourself
- When you become defensive, you stop listening.
- Offence causes separation, it's like a wall (or a fence) is created between people by disagreement and conflict
- You must be honest with each other, acknowledge each other
- Value people, all are created in the the Lord's image and likeness (Genesis 1:26)
- Being calm and keeping your voice down will help communication
- By listening you show that the other persons opinion is valued and that their voice matters
- Pick your battles, some things are important to say, others are not
- Some things you will need to make a stand for
- Love not hatred and anger. Violence is never the answer!
- Forgiveness not only sets them free, but you too ...
- You are who Jesus says you are, not who they say you are

Keys to handle conflict situations:

- Remain calm and keep an open mind, a closed mind will prevent resolution
- Listen to what the other person has to say
- Understand their perspective
- Commit together to working it out
- In order for you to be right, they don't have to be wrong
- You can always agree to disagree but do so without carrying hurt or anger inside
- There is no need to keep defending yourself
- Learn to forgive others, no one is perfect
- Give yourself time to think, you do not have to conclude disagreements immediately
- Keep communication open, healing relationships can take time
- Seek help from trusted and experienced mediators
- Pray for them, hand them over to our loving Heavenly Father

SESSION 8: RESOLVING CONFLICT

 PARTICIPATION

Tick which apply to you because of unresolved conflict with another person:

- ☐ Felt misunderstood (confusion, sadness, alone …)
- ☐ Felt that you reacted in a wrong way (reaction, angry, defensive…)
- ☐ Felt offended (hurt, blame, shame…)
- ☐ Felt that they should apologise first (stubborn …)
- ☐ Lost a friendship (loss…)
- ☐ Separated from a family member (isolated …)
- ☐ Had your heart hurt (emotional…)
- ☐ Got into a fight (physical…)
- ☐ Wished you could have another chance (cut off…)
- ☐ Felt lied about (gossip…)
- ☐ Other _____

Name people you have conflicted with that you would like to have acted differently:

_____

_____

_____

Select either YES or NO for each statement below:

YES	NO	
___	___	I get angry easily
___	___	I struggle to listen to other peoples' perspectives or opinions
___	___	I would rather avoid conflict than address the issue
___	___	I don't like to admit I am wrong
___	___	I find it hard to say I am sorry
___	___	I react without thinking, get frustrated or defensive
___	___	I want to change how I handle conflict with others
___	___	I believe different opinions can exist together
___	___	Admitting when I am wrong is a strength, not a weakness

SESSION 8: RESOLVING CONFLICT

 SCRIPTURES

Psalms 145:8
The LORD is gracious and full of compassion,
Slow to anger and great in mercy.

Proverbs 12:18
There is one who speaks like the piercings of a sword,
But the tongue of the wise promotes health.

Matthew 18:15
if your brother sins against you, go and tell him his fault between you and him alone.
If he hears you, you have gained your brother.

James 1:19
let every man be swift to hear, slow to speak, slow to wrath [anger, vengeance];

Proverbs 15:1
A soft answer turns away wrath, But a harsh word stirs up anger.

Matthew 5:9
Blessed are the peacemakers, For they shall be called sons of God.

Colossians 3:13
bearing with one another, and forgiving one another, if anyone has a complaint against another;
even as Christ forgave you, so you also must do.

SESSION 8: RESOLVING CONFLICT

 FACILITATOR DISCUSSION POINTS

Discuss: How water is formless, so too is Living Water formless, ready to fill all shapes and vessels.

- ❖ Water fills containers and takes on new shapes, without losing its identity
- ❖ Be like water and flow together, being confident in who you are
- ❖ You can overcome conflict by being flexible
- ❖ To compromise won't change who you are and what you believe
- ❖ Every part you give over to the Lord, He will fill with Living Water

Discuss: What is CANCEL CULTURE in the world today.

Cancel culture : Oxford Learners Dictionary:

… the practice of excluding somebody from social or professional life by refusing to communicate with them online or in real life, because they have said or done something that other people do not agree with

Discuss: Forgiveness, sets us free.

- ❖ Forgiveness brings spiritual, emotional and physical healing
- ❖ Talk about forgiving others, and the impact it has on you
- ❖ Talk about finding forgiveness for others even when they are not sorry … letting it go

SESSION 8: RESOLVING CONFLICT

 PRAYER

Session 8 Prayer is based on the LORD'S Prayer in Matthew 6:7-13

HEAVENLY FATHER,

Your Name is Holy, Mighty and Powerful,

thank you that You are able to transform me from the inside out.

Help me with my relationships.

Especially the people that I have unresolved conflict with.

May Your Kingdom increase in me,

as I look carefully at myself in the mirror of Your reflection.

Reveal to me what needs to shift in me,

so I can represent You well

and not be so hurt and offended in disagreements and conflict.

Let Your Holy Spirit rule and reign in me,

fill me with Your anointing.

May Your will be magnified through me,

as I choose to behave like You,

even when others don't understand me, reject me or try to cancel me,

or say unfair things to me or about me.

Thank you for each precious day, You are the Bread of LIFE, our daily bread.

Forgive my sins, hurts, unforgiveness and anger towards others,

as I forgive others for how they have upset and hurt me.

I will not be tempted anymore with unforgiveness … I forgive them,

I hand each person, every conflict situation, into Your Holy, Mighty and Powerful Hands…

Protect me from the evil one,

heal me and restore me as I forgive them.

You alone deserve the Glory for Your healing hand upon my life.

For Yours is the Kingdom and the power and the glory, forever and ever.

AMEN

SESSION 8: RESOLVING CONFLICT

 NOTES

Please use the space below to write down comments, thoughts, ideas, pictures etc …as our Heavenly Father shows you important things for your life…

SESSION 9: FLOW LIKE A RIVER

"PERMISSION TO TRY AGAIN"

The Lord's mercies … are new every morning.
Lamentations 3:22-23

SESSION 9: FLOW LIKE A RIVER

OBJECTIVES

- Many of us feel snagged and left behind by life
- To flow, means letting go of the things that hold you back, and moving forward with the flow of new things ahead … the healing of the broken hearted
- It's time to try again
- Forgiving yourself is key

KEY CONCEPTS

- Many of us want to step forward, but somehow, we can't do it
- The desire is there, to succeed and we may even know what to do, but we can't
- It's like an invisible force grabs you and slows you down
- Like there is conflict inside yourself, as though your inner thoughts or conscience is conflicting with your behaviour
- You know what is right but you are struggling to do what is right …
- The weight of certain situations can cause a sense of paralysis that stop you from moving forward
- It's like you have been snagged or hooked by a branch and you are no longer able to flow with the WATERS OF LIFE
- Other people have perhaps passed you by and you feel loss at being left behind

To flow again, means letting go of the things that are holding you back, and moving forward with the flow of new things ahead.

- Not only is it a healing inside
- A permission to proceed
- A worthiness to receive
- But also a letting go of control and a resting in the Lord
- Let go and let God work with and for you
- Letting go of negative words, hurts, disappointments, insecurities, unforgiveness …
- You can't change your past, but you can shape your future, together with Him

Forgiving yourself, is critical and often not discussed.

- ❖ Forgiving people and unfair circumstances is one thing, having the strength to pick yourself up and try again is something else altogether
- ❖ To achieve this, it's important to forgive YOURSELF, and give yourself permission to try again
- ❖ You are made in His image and likeness, He does not make mistakes
- ❖ The enemy of God, the devil somehow attacks us in our areas of gifting
- ❖ In other words, the gift that our Heavenly Father has placed in you, the uniqueness in you, your specific identity ... comes under attack
- ❖ Good News: as you stand up under these attacks, you strengthen and overcome the attacks, ultimately bursting forth and launching into your Heavenly Destiny

How to flow in the River of Life, and pursue your Heavenly Destiny.

- ❖ Make the LORD the centre of your life
- ❖ Hold His hand tightly, and everything else lightly
- ❖ Seek our Heavenly Father's counsel for His path ahead for you, His way is best
- ❖ To flow like a river, means to be set free
- ❖ The LORD is the River of Life
- ❖ He turns our hearts from feeling dry, empty, hopeless and blocked, into rivers of Living Water and we never thirst again
- ❖ It's not important what others think about you

 EXERCISE:

Driving a car: Talk about the following together as a group.

- ▸ What you constantly look at, can define the direction you travel
- ▸ By looking forward at the new path ahead, you will move in that direction
- ▸ By constantly looking back at the past, it will be harder to move forward with freedom
- ▸ You cannot drive a car while looking out the back window, or staring in the rear view mirror
- ▸ Then you will either stop going forward, or perhaps crash
- ▸ The rear view mirrors are important because they are there to look at briefly, to reflect and ensure safety
- ▸ Look forward to your Heavenly Fathers plan, your Heavenly Destiny and live in expectation of what is to come
- ▸ Don't live in the past, where you cannot change things

SESSION 9: FLOW LIKE A RIVER

 PARTICIPATION

Tick the following statements that apply to you:

- [ ] There has been an invisible force holding me back (paralysed inside) for some time
- [ ] I often judge myself harshly
- [ ] I have not been happy with who I am, how I look and/or with how I behave
- [ ] It feels like others are better than me
- [ ] I have felt sad, depressed, angry, lost, hurt … left behind … snagged
- [ ] I acknowledge that I am made in the image and likeness of the Lord (Gen 1:26)
- [ ] The Lord does not make mistakes
- [ ] I know that I need to forgive myself in order to set myself free
- [ ] My opinion of me matters
- [ ] The Lord's opinion of me matters
- [ ] What others think of me does not matter
- [ ] It's time to flow like a river

Write down the things that you need to forgive yourself for:

_____

_____

_____

DECLARATION OF PERSONAL FORGIVENESS

Today I forgive myself …

- I acknowledge that I have made mistakes
- I am made in His image and likeness,
- I am not a mistake
- I ask the Lord to forgive me for judging myself
- Today I give myself permission to try again

Name: _____

Date: _____

Signature: _____

SESSION 9: FLOW LIKE A RIVER

 SCRIPTURES

Isaiah 43:19
Behold, I will do a new thing, Now it shall spring forth;
Shall you not know it?
I will even make a road in the wilderness, And rivers in the desert.

John 4:14
but whoever drinks of the water that I shall give him will never thirst. But the water that I shall give him will become in him a fountain of water springing up into everlasting life."

Psalms 34:18
The LORD is near to those who have a broken heart …

Psalms 147:3
He heals the broken-hearted
And binds up their wounds.

John 14:6
Jesus said to him, "I am the way, the truth, and the life. No one comes to the Father except through Me.

John 3:5
Jesus answered, "Most assuredly, I say to you, unless one is born of water and the Spirit, he cannot enter the kingdom of God.

Revelation 22:1
And he showed me a pure river of water of life, clear as crystal, proceeding from the throne of God and of the Lamb.

Lamentations 3:22-23
The Lord's mercies … are new every morning.

SESSION 9: FLOW LIKE A RIVER

 FACILITATOR DISCUSSION POINTS

Discuss: The EXERCISE **Driving a car**

Discuss: These important concepts.

- ❖ To flow like a river, means to be set free
- ❖ The LORD is the River of Life, be filled to overflowing

Discuss: The concept of FORGIVING YOURSELF, in relation to the following.

- ❖ In Session 8, we discussed forgiving others … but forgiving yourself is important too
- ❖ What does it means to forgive yourself and how does it impact you?
- ❖ You are human, and we all make mistakes, right?
- ❖ Give yourself permission to try again

Discuss: The RIVER OF LIFE

- ❖ When you drink from the River of Life, you never thirst again: because it's a supernatural river (John 4:14)
- ❖ Jesus is the only path to freedom, He is the Way, the Truth and the Life (John 14:6)

SESSION 9: FLOW LIKE A RIVER

 PRAYER

HEAVENLY FATHER,

You are the true River of Life.

Let Your supernatural River of Life ,

transform the desert areas within me.

Heal my heart Lord.

Release me into my Heavenly Destiny.

It's at Your throne that I find The River of Living Water,

wash me clean, cleanse my heart,

and restore me from the burdens that I have been carrying.

I lay them down at Your throne.

I ask You to forgive me as I forgive MYSELF,

let me see myself through Your eyes,

created in Your Image and Likeness.

You are my Father,

help me to accept myself.

Heal my past and take my hand,

as You lead me into my future.

Thank you for never giving up on me

I am a new creation … Your new creation,

washed clean by the perfect work of the Cross of Calvary.

Thank you for making a way for me.

You take my heart of stone and give me a heart of flesh.

You bind up the brokenhearted,

for You truly are Loving Kindness.

Renew my mind, and lead me to the river of transformation.

In Jesus Name,

AMEN

SESSION 9: FLOW LIKE A RIVER

 NOTES

Please use the space below to write down comments, thoughts, ideas, pictures etc …as our Heavenly Father shows you important things for your life…

SESSION 10: STEPPING OUT IN FAITH

"STEP INTO YOUR HEAVENLY DESTINY"

The voice of the LORD is over the waters; The God of Glory thunders; The LORD is over many waters.

Psalms 29:3

SESSION 10: STEPPING OUT IN FAITH

OBJECTIVES

- ❖ Your life matters greatly, live it with passion
- ❖ Setting your life vision
- ❖ Your Heavenly Destiny
- ❖ It all starts with stepping out in faith
- ❖ Walking on water

Three steps towards your Heavenly Destiny (2 Timothy 1:7)

- ❖ **Love** (Father)
- ❖ **Power** (Holy Spirit)
- ❖ **Sound Mind** (Mind of Christ)
- ❖ A Spirit… One Spirit in you … The Father, Son and Holy Spirit are ONE
- ❖ Faith is the opposite of fear

KEY CONCEPTS

- ❖ Stepping out in faith … doing something new, takes faith
- ❖ Create momentum through achievable goals … work within your limitations, take small steps often
- ❖ Being brave and honest with yourself and be accountable to others
- ❖ Stay focused, avoiding distractions and temptations that can take you off track
- ❖ You must believe in Him and believe in who He has made you to be
- ❖ We each need to take a step towards our future, our Heavenly Destiny
- ❖ It's time to step out of the boat, and walk on water
- ❖ You are a Champion; greatness is before you
- ❖ It all starts with stepping out in faith, believing in His plan for you
- ❖ Jesus calls us out onto the spiritual water
- ❖ His voice is upon the many waters
- ❖ You are important, look up, take His hand, look forward, GO!
- ❖ Do this in FAITH trusting Him, don't respond in FEAR

- Faith is the evidence of things hoped for … what are you hoping for, set your path
- We make our plans, but the Lord orders our steps, when we do it together
- Faith in action, you are worthy of a better future (Ephesians 3:20)
- Use your past as a launchpad into your future
- It's time to start dreaming again, to take hold of your Heavenly Destiny
- Imagine it, write it down … VISION
- Heavenly desires, come from the Lord
- You have released the weight and burdens, it's time to step out in faith
- Empowered by Fathers River of Life, from Him to us, from us to others … connected as ONE
- Fruit of the spirit (love, joy, peace, patience, kindness, goodness, faithfulness, gentleness, self-control … Galatians 5:22)
- The Lord is calling you to step over and trust Him
- Greatness is in you, through Jesus our Lord and Saviour

SESSION 10: STEPPING OUT IN FAITH

 **EXRECISE:**

Please read Matthew 14:22-33 together

(Jesus Walks on the Water- Amplified Version)

Immediately He directed the disciples to get into the boat and go ahead of Him to the other side [of the Sea of Galilee], while He sent the crowds away.

After He had dismissed the crowds, He went up on the mountain by Himself to pray. When it was evening, He was there alone.

But the boat [by this time] was already a long distance from land, tossed and battered by the waves; for the wind was against them. And in the fourth watch of the night (3:00-6:00 a.m.) Jesus came to them, walking on the sea.

When the disciples saw Him walking on the sea, they were terrified, and said, "It is a ghost!" And they cried out in fear. But immediately He spoke to them, saying, "Take courage, it is I! Do not be afraid!"

Peter replied to Him, "Lord, if it is [really] You, command me to come to You on the water." He said, "Come!" So Peter got out of the boat, and walked on the water and came toward Jesus.

But when he saw [the effects of] the wind, he was frightened, and he began to sink, and he cried out, "Lord, save me!"

Immediately Jesus extended His hand and caught him, saying to him, "O you of little faith, why did you doubt?" And when they got into the boat, the wind ceased.

Then those in the boat worshiped Him [with awe-inspired reverence], saying, "Truly You are the Son of God!"

SESSION 10: STEPPING OUT IN FAITH

 PARTICIPATION

Please read the scripture: Matthew 14:22-33 together as a group.

Using this scripture, apply the key imagery of the story to your life and answer the following questions:

1. They (disciples) had left to sail to the other side, what does the other side symbolise to you and your current situation?

   _____

   (write above: … it could symbolise any 'destination or goal' that needs to be achieved)

2. What could the boat symbolise for you?

   _____

   (write above: … … it could symbolise the first step you must take to get onto the water)

3. What does the storm symbolise to you?

   _____

   (write above: … … it could symbolise a trial or difficulty that challenges your faith)

4. Like Peter, we can get out of the boat onto the (spiritual) water, what does it mean for you to take His hand in your life?

   _____

   (write above: … to trust Jesus, have faith in Him, with your trial, hurt, pain, fears, future …)

5. *What does YOUR Heavenly Destiny look like?*

   _____

   (write above: … Use your imagination, picture it, write it down, your VISION)

SESSION 10: STEPPING OUT IN FAITH

 SCRIPTURES:

2 Timothy 1:7
For God has not given us a spirit of fear, but of power and of love and of a sound mind.

1 Corinthians 6:17
But he who is joined to the Lord is one spirit with Him.

Psalms 29:3
The voice of the LORD is over the waters; The God of glory thunders;
The LORD is over many waters.

1 John 5:14
Now this is the confidence that we have in Him, that if we ask anything according to His will, He hears us.

Mark 9:23
Jesus said to him, "If you can believe, all things are possible to him who believes."

Hebrews 11:1
Now faith is the substance of things hoped for, the evidence of things not seen.

Proverbs 16:9
A man's heart plans his way, But the LORD directs his steps.

Ephesians 3:20 AMP
Now to Him who is able to [carry out His purpose and] do superabundantly more than all that we dare ask or think [infinitely beyond our greatest prayers, hopes, or dreams], according to His power that is at work within us,

Psalms 37:4
Delight yourself also in the LORD,
And He shall give you the desires of your heart.

Psalms 37:5
Commit your way to the LORD,
Trust also in Him, And He shall bring it to pass.

Romans 5:5
Now hope does not disappoint, because the love of God has been poured out in our hearts by the Holy Spirit who was given to us.

SESSION 10: STEPPING OUT IN FAITH

 FACILITATOR DISCUSSION POINTS

Discuss: Please read the following and then discuss with the Participants.

- Just like Peter did, when he stepped out onto water, you too can step out in faith into the place that Jesus is calling you to
- They set sail from the shore and Jesus appeared later walking on water
- During rough seas Jesus called Peter to climb out of the boat and join Him walking on water
- Jesus calls you out onto the water too …
- The water is a new dimension of the Spirit
- It's a place you step into by faith
- It's linked to your Heavenly Destiny
- It's one thing launching out in a boat from the shore,
- It's another thing altogether, stepping out of the boat by faith, onto the water of the Spirit

Discuss: Give opportunity for Participants to share what they have learned from RIVER FLOW.

SESSION 10: STEPPING OUT IN FAITH

 PRAYER

HEAVENLY FATHER,

> You are the true River of Life,
>
> lead me deep into Your Living Waters of New Life.
>
> As I step forward boldly, trusting You,
>
> I take Your hand tightly, in faith …
>
> I hold everything else lightly, in faith …
>
> Knowing that You are the Author and Perfecter of my faith.
>
> You are the centre of all things,
>
> and You are my Heavenly Father.
>
> I declare that I no longer have a contract with the devil,
>
> I rejoice that I have a covenant with You, Lord Almighty,
>
> written in Your Blood … Your Blood has set me free.
>
> I command the enemy of the Lord, the devil to … GET OUT …
>
> Get out of my body, soul and spirit.
>
> I have been set free, and who the Lord sets free, is free indeed.
>
> Mighty Lord, I receive Your incredible healing for my soul … my mind, will and emotions.
>
> I surrender to Your Perfect Love, that casts out fear.
>
> Greater are You in me, than he who is in the world.
>
> I praise Your Holy Name that I am no longer bound by darkness.
>
> I give You all the Glory for Your great Power has redeemed me.
>
> I belong with You … I am hidden in You.
>
> I look ahead and rejoice at our partnership, walking together for Your Glory
>
> Magnify Your divine light through me,
>
> let Your Peace rest upon me,
>
> And may Your Joy be my Strength, forever.
>
> In Jesus Name,

AMEN

SESSION 10: STEPPING OUT IN FAITH

 NOTES

Please use the space below to write down comments, thoughts, ideas, pictures etc …as our Heavenly Father shows you important things for your life…

THANK YOU AND ADDITIONAL RESOURCES

THANK YOU

Thank you for the time you have invested in yourself through RIVER FLOW™, we hope and trust that it has been life changing for you and that your new life of freedom and faith will take you forward and you will reach out boldly and take hold of your Heavenly Destiny.

Please share RIVER FLOW™ with others, so their lives can also be enriched.

ADDITIONAL RESOURCES

RIVER FLOW™ videos can be found at: www.riverflowinternational.com.au

RIVER FLOW™ Donations can be made at: https://donorbox.org/river-flow-support

RIVER FLOW™ DEVOTIONAL: in production, will keep you posted

About the Author, Chris Millin : www.chrismillin.com.au

Verandah Church App (free …IOS and Android) : https://subsplash.com/jirehseedltd/app

Jireh Seed Ministries : www.jirehseed.org

DONATE HERE

https://donorbox.org/river-flow-support